Churchill's Blueprint: **Leading in the Modern World**

Paul A Hopper & James 'Max' Sanchez

Churchill's Blueprint: Leading in the Modern World

Embark on a transformative journey with Winston Churchill in "Churchill's Blueprint: Leading in the Modern World." Discover the keys to exceptional leadership as you explore the life and legacy of one of history's greatest leaders. Uncover Churchill's resilience in the face of adversity and learn how to navigate challenges with unwavering determination. Gain insights into his strategic decision-making and master the art of effective communication to inspire and influence others.

Explore the power of teamwork and collaboration in diverse environments. Discover strategies for fostering unity and driving innovation in the modern workplace.

Navigate change with agility and embrace strategic leadership principles to guide your organization through turbulent times. Learn the importance of integrity and ethical leadership, making principled decisions that inspire trust and create a positive impact. Reflect on Churchill's lasting legacy and discover how you can leave your own mark on the future. Unleash your leadership potential and shape the world with purpose, passion, and unwavering commitment.

"Churchill's Blueprint: Leading in the Modern World" is your essential guide to unlocking leadership greatness. Prepare to be inspired and equipped with practical tools to navigate the complexities of the modern landscape and make a lasting difference. Step into the footsteps of Winston Churchill and uncover the blueprint for leadership success. Are you ready to embrace the challenge and leave an indelible mark on the world? The journey begins now.

Winston Churchill, a renowned British statesman and Prime Minister, left an indelible mark on history through his exceptional leadership during World War II and his profound impact on global politics. "Churchill's Blueprint: Leading in the Modern World" delves into Churchill's extraordinary life and distills his timeless lessons, offering guidance for leaders in navigating the complexities of the contemporary era.

Sir Winston Churchill (1874-1965) was a British politician, statesman, and renowned orator. Born into an aristocratic family, Churchill embarked on a remarkable political career that spanned over six decades. He served as Prime Minister of the United Kingdom twice, from 1940 to 1945 and from 1951 to 1955, and held numerous other important positions in the British government.

Churchill's leadership during World War II is particularly notable. His resolute determination and inspiring speeches rallied the British people during their darkest hours, elevating their morale and steering the nation towards victory. Churchill's unwavering commitment to the Allied cause and his ability to make tough decisions in times of crisis cemented his status as an iconic world leader.

Throughout his life, Churchill demonstrated qualities that remain relevant today, such as resilience in the face of adversity, strategic thinking, effective communication, and the ability to inspire and unite people. His legacy extends far beyond his wartime leadership, encompassing his contributions to literature, historical writing, and public service.

"Churchill's Blueprint: Leading in the Modern World" draws upon Churchill's experiences, insights, and triumphs, distilling his wisdom into practical lessons for leaders in today's complex and rapidly changing world. The book offers a compelling exploration of Churchill's life, highlighting his relevance as a guiding figure for contemporary leadership.

The Relevance of "Churchill's Blueprint: Leading in the Modern World"

In today's rapidly evolving and complex world, the wisdom of Winston Churchill holds tremendous value for individuals, leaders, and business entrepreneurs. "Churchill's Blueprint: Leading in the Modern World" serves as a guidebook, drawing from Churchill's remarkable life lessons and leadership principles to offer practical insights for navigating contemporary challenges. This book holds profound significance for various audiences, and here's why:

For the Modern Individual

In an era marked by uncertainty, fast-paced changes, and personal aspirations, individuals often find themselves searching for guidance on how to succeed and lead meaningful lives. Churchill's life exemplifies resilience, determination, and adaptability—qualities that resonate with modern individuals seeking personal growth, self-belief, and the ability to overcome obstacles. By exploring Churchill's experiences and applying his insights, readers can gain valuable lessons on perseverance, courage, and visionary thinking, empowering them to thrive in their personal endeavors.

For Leaders

Effective leadership is crucial across various domains, from politics and business to community initiatives and social movements. Churchill's extraordinary leadership during World War II and his strategic decision-making abilities offer invaluable lessons for leaders today. By studying Churchill's approach to leadership, readers can enhance their own skills in inspiring and guiding teams, making tough decisions in times of crisis, and maintaining unwavering determination in the face of adversity. Churchill's blueprint for leadership serves as a guiding light for those aspiring to lead with integrity, inspire others, and leave a lasting positive impact.

For Business Entrepreneurs

Entrepreneurship in the modern world requires more than just a good idea—it demands resilience, innovation, adaptability, and effective communication. Churchill's life serves as a source of inspiration for business entrepreneurs seeking to build successful ventures and make a meaningful difference. By examining Churchill's visionary thinking, embracing change, and ability to unite diverse groups, entrepreneurs can gain fresh perspectives and strategies for navigating the challenges of the business landscape. The book offers insights into creating a resilient entrepreneurial mindset, making courageous decisions, and leaving a lasting legacy.

"Churchill's Blueprint: Leading in the Modern World" is not merely a historical account but a guidebook for personal growth, leadership development, and entrepreneurial success. By exploring Churchill's experiences and drawing parallels to contemporary contexts, this book empowers readers to apply Churchill's principles and wisdom to their own lives, careers, and ventures. Through the lens of Churchill's remarkable journey, readers will discover the timeless relevance and transformative potential of his teachings.

As we embark on this writing journey, we will delve into the specific chapters that explore Churchill's lessons in detail, offering practical advice and actionable strategies. Together, we will inspire readers to embrace their potential, overcome challenges, and lead with purpose in the modern world.

Let's proceed to the first chapter—"The Art of Perseverance: Thriving in the Face of Adversity."

Contents

CHAPTER 9:47

"Legacy and Impact: Leaving a Lasting Mark on the Future"

CHAPTER 1

The Art of Perseverance: Thriving in the Face of Adversity

In the vast tapestry of human history, certain individuals emerge as beacons of resilience, their stories etched into the annals of time. One such luminary is Winston Churchill, a titan of leadership and an unwavering symbol of perseverance. From the depths of personal setbacks to the crucible of global conflict, Churchill's indomitable spirit shines as a guiding light, illuminating the path for those who seek to thrive in the face of adversity.

As we embark on this remarkable journey, we find ourselves captivated by the allure of Churchill's life—a life that encapsulates the full spectrum of human experience, from soaring triumphs to soul-wrenching tribulations. Through the lens of his extraordinary journey, we unravel the threads of resilience, extracting wisdom and practical strategies that resonate with our own modern challenges.

The tales of Churchill's struggles and triumphs weave a tapestry of inspiration, evoking a profound sense of admiration and curiosity. How did he find the strength to persist when the world seemed to conspire against him? What strategies did he employ to maintain unwavering determination in the face of seemingly insurmountable obstacles? These questions beckon us to delve deep into the recesses of Churchill's life, unearthing the secrets of his resilience and the lessons they hold for us all.

As we embark on this expedition, we shall bear witness to the crucible of Churchill's personal hardships—the political defeats that would have shattered the resolve of most, the bouts of depression that threatened to engulf his spirit, and the personal tragedies that etched scars upon his soul. Yet, through it all, Churchill emerged as a towering figure, resolute and unyielding.

But this is not merely a historical account, for the true value of Churchill's story lies in its enduring relevance. In the tumultuous landscape of the modern world, where challenges abound and uncertainties loom, the lessons of resilience gleaned from Churchill's life take on a renewed significance. We stand on the precipice of a journey that will navigate not only the depths of Churchill's struggles but also the heights of his victories, seeking to distill his wisdom into practical strategies that can empower us all.

In the chapters that follow, we shall delve into the intricacies of Churchill's art of perseverance. We will explore the essence of his resilience, drawing upon real-life scenarios from his tumultuous journey to illuminate our own paths. We will discover strategies for maintaining unwavering motivation, overcoming obstacles with determination, and cultivating a support network that bolsters our spirit.

But as we embark upon this exploration, let us leave you on the edge of anticipation, for the true power of Churchill's resilience lies not merely in the lessons we uncover, but in the transformation they can evoke within ourselves. In the chapters to come, we shall unveil the layers of Churchill's blueprint for leading in the modern world. Brace yourself, for this is but the beginning of a profound journey that will forever alter the way you perceive challenges and ignite the flame of resilience within your own soul.

The winds of destiny beckon us forward. Are you ready to embark on this transformative expedition?

Unveiling Churchill's Resilience: We dive into the depths of Churchill's life, tracing the contours of his remarkable story. From his early political failures to the monumental trials of World War II, we witness the unyielding spirit and determination that defined Churchill's character. Through his example, we gain a profound understanding of the power of resilience.

Extracting Lessons from Churchill's Journey: We immerse ourselves in Churchill's experiences, extracting profound lessons that resonate with our own lives. We explore how Churchill approached adversity as an opportunity for growth and harnessed his indomitable spirit to face challenges head-on. By delving into the nuances of his journey, we uncover wisdom that can guide us through our own trials and tribulations.

Strategies for Sustaining Motivation: Thriving in the modern world necessitates the ability to maintain motivation even in the most challenging circumstances. Inspired by Churchill's resilience, we delve into practical strategies that can fuel our own motivation. From cultivating a positive mindset to discovering personal purpose and setting achievable goals, we equip ourselves with the tools to sustain our drive in the face of adversity.

Navigating Obstacles with Determination: Churchill's tenacity in overcoming obstacles serves as a beacon of inspiration. We explore how he approached challenges, adapted to changing circumstances, and found innovative solutions. By delving into real-life scenarios from Churchill's life and drawing parallels to our own challenges, we gain invaluable insights into effective problem-solving and navigating obstacles with unwavering determination.

The Power of a Support Network: No journey of perseverance can be traversed in isolation. Churchill's life teaches us the importance of building a robust support network. We delve into the relationships that played pivotal roles in Churchill's life and leadership, emphasizing the strength and guidance derived from such alliances. By cultivating our own support systems, seeking guidance, and fostering collaboration, we enhance our ability to endure and thrive.

Resilient Leadership: Churchill's resilience extended beyond personal struggles, shaping his remarkable leadership style. We examine how his ability to persevere influenced his leadership during times of crisis and uncertainty. Drawing from his example, we delve into strategies for inspiring resilience within teams and organizations, equipping leaders with the tools to navigate challenging environments and guide their teams towards success.

In this opening chapter, we have embarked on a profound exploration of the art of perseverance, drawing inspiration from Winston Churchill's extraordinary life. By delving into Churchill's journey, we have uncovered invaluable strategies for maintaining motivation and overcoming obstacles in the modern world. As we continue our expedition through the remaining chapters, we will deepen our understanding of Churchill's blueprint for leadership and personal growth in the face of adversity.

CHAPTER 2
Courageous Decision-Making: Navigating Complexity with Confidence

In this chapter, we embark on a captivating exploration of Winston Churchill's remarkable ability to make courageous decisions amidst complex and uncertain circumstances. Churchill's life was marked by critical moments that demanded resolute action and unwavering conviction. We delve into these pivotal junctures, analyzing his bold decision-making and extracting valuable lessons that can guide us in navigating the intricate challenges of the modern world.

Crucible of Decision-Making; The weight of responsibility rested heavily on Churchill's shoulders during World War II and other crucial moments in his life. We delve into the crucible of decision-making that he faced, examining the magnitude of the choices before him. From the daunting task of leading a nation at war to the complexities of diplomatic negotiations, we explore how Churchill's unwavering resolve and strategic thinking enabled him to make decisive and impactful choices.

Decisiveness in the Face of Adversity; Churchill's ability to remain decisive in the face of adversity becomes a source of inspiration. We delve into his unyielding determination, analyzing how he confronted seemingly insurmountable challenges head-on. Through gripping accounts, we explore how Churchill's resolute decision-making helped him navigate political obstacles, military campaigns, and personal setbacks, instilling confidence and rallying others in times of crisis.

Embracing Calculated Risk; Churchill was no stranger to taking calculated risks when necessary. We examine how he balanced the potential rewards against the inherent uncertainties in critical situations. Drawing from historical examples, we analyze Churchill's strategic thinking and his ability to assess risks with a clear understanding of the potential consequences. By understanding his calculated risk-taking approach, we gain insights into how to evaluate risks in our own lives and make informed decisions with confidence.

Strategies for Sound Decision-Making; Effective decision-making requires a comprehensive toolkit of strategies. Inspired by Churchill's decision-making prowess, we explore techniques that can enhance our own abilities. We delve into the importance of gathering and analyzing information from diverse sources, considering multiple perspectives, and weighing potential outcomes. By developing a holistic framework for sound decision-making, we empower ourselves to make informed choices that stand the test of time.

Harnessing Intuition and Gut Feelings; In addition to rational analysis, Churchill recognized the value of intuition and gut feelings in decision-making. We examine how he honed his instincts and listened to his inner voice when faced with complex situations. Through insightful anecdotes, we explore the integration of rationality and intuition, allowing us to tap into our own intuition as a valuable tool for decision-making.

As we conclude this chapter on courageous decision-making, we marvel at Churchill's ability to navigate complexity with unwavering confidence. From the crucible of critical moments to embracing calculated risks, Churchill's life provides invaluable lessons for modern decision-makers. By studying his approach and incorporating the strategies discussed, we equip ourselves with the tools to make sound decisions and lead with conviction in an ever-changing world.

The path forward is illuminated by the courage to decide. Will you embrace the lessons of Churchill's decision-making prowess and step boldly into the challenges that lie ahead? Stay tuned as we uncover more of Churchill's blueprint for leading in the modern world.

[To be continued...]

CHAPTER 3
Mastering Communication: Inspiring and Influencing Others

In this captivating chapter, we immerse ourselves in the realm of Winston Churchill's extraordinary communication skills—a cornerstone of his influential leadership. Churchill's ability to inspire and influence others through his powerful oratory and persuasive style is a testament to his profound impact on history.

We delve deep into the techniques that made Churchill's speeches resonate with audiences, transcending time and leaving an enduring legacy. Through the strategic use of rhetoric, he crafted compelling arguments that stirred emotions and ignited a sense of purpose. By mastering the art of storytelling, Churchill weaved narratives that captivated listeners, painting vivid pictures of hope and determination.

However, effective communication is not solely about words. We explore the essence of authenticity, recognizing that genuine connections are built on sincerity and transparency. Churchill's empathy and ability to relate to people from all walks of life serve as a powerful lesson. By actively listening and understanding the perspectives of others, we cultivate empathy and bridge divides, fostering unity and collaboration.

Nonverbal communication also played a significant role in Churchill's commanding presence. We examine his confident body language, expressive gestures, and unwavering gaze, understanding the impact of nonverbal cues in conveying conviction and authority. By harnessing the power of our own nonverbal communication, we amplify our messages and deepen their resonance. In today's digital age, virtual communication has become increasingly prevalent. We navigate the intricacies of connecting authentically through screens, adapting our communication styles to online platforms. We explore the possibilities offered by technology, leveraging its tools to convey our messages with clarity and impact. From virtual presentations to online collaborations, we seize the opportunities presented by the digital landscape to reach diverse audiences and make a difference.

As we traverse this chapter, we draw inspiration from Churchill's timeless communication legacy. His ability to inspire and influence others remains a guiding light in the modern world. By mastering the art of communication, we unlock our own potential to captivate hearts, inspire action, and shape a better future.

CHAPTER 4
Building Effective Teams: Collaboration and Unity in a Diverse World

In this captivating chapter, we delve deep into the extraordinary leadership of Winston Churchill, exploring his unparalleled ability to build effective teams that thrive on collaboration and unity amidst diversity. Churchill recognized the immense power of bringing together individuals with different backgrounds, perspectives, and talents, understanding that it is through the collective strength of a cohesive team that great achievements are made.

Drawing inspiration from Churchill's remarkable leadership during World War II, we unravel the principles that underpinned his approach to team building. As Prime Minister, he faced the daunting task of uniting people from various political parties, military branches, and social backgrounds, forging a sense of shared purpose and determination. We study his strategies for creating an environment of trust, respect, and open communication, where each team member's contribution was valued and encouraged.

At the heart of effective teamwork lies the recognition and embrace of diversity. Churchill fostered an inclusive culture where diverse perspectives were celebrated and actively sought after. We explore strategies for cultivating inclusivity in the modern workplace, where individuals from different backgrounds can thrive and contribute their unique insights. By encouraging constructive debates and embracing dissenting opinions, we unlock the power of diverse thinking, enabling teams to arrive at innovative solutions and make informed decisions.

Central to successful collaboration is effective communication and a shared vision. We analyze Churchill's ability to articulate a compelling vision that inspired and aligned his team members toward a common goal. By studying his approach to communicating goals and expectations, we gain insights into how to foster a sense of shared purpose and commitment in our own teams. Furthermore, we delve into techniques for creating a collaborative environment where ideas are freely shared, and active listening fosters mutual understanding.

Strong relationships and trust form the foundation of high-performing teams. Churchill invested time and effort in understanding his team members, recognizing their strengths and aspirations. We explore his leadership techniques, including building rapport, resolving conflicts, and motivating individuals to reach their full potential. By creating a supportive and empowering environment, we enable our teams to flourish and achieve exceptional results.

In today's digital landscape, remote collaboration has become increasingly prevalent. We examine the challenges and opportunities presented by virtual teamwork, exploring how technology can facilitate meaningful connections across geographical boundaries. From virtual team meetings to online project management, we navigate the intricacies of remote collaboration, ensuring that our teams remain connected, engaged, and productive.

As we conclude this chapter, we reflect on Churchill's enduring legacy as a master team builder. His principles of embracing diversity, fostering collaboration, and cultivating unity are as relevant today as ever. By leveraging the collective intelligence and unique strengths of our teams, we can overcome challenges, drive innovation, and create a better future together.

CHAPTER 5
Strategic Leadership: Guiding Through Turbulent Times

In this expansive and enlightening chapter, we embark on a profound exploration of Winston Churchill's strategic leadership during times of immense crisis. Churchill's remarkable ability to navigate through turbulent waters, make bold decisions, and inspire hope in the face of adversity serves as a timeless example of effective leadership. As we delve deeper into his strategic thinking and decision-making, we uncover invaluable insights that can guide us through the complexities of the modern world.

Churchill's words echo through history, resonating with the challenges we face today: "The empires of the future are the empires of the mind." This profound quote encapsulates his visionary thinking and the recognition that true leadership extends beyond the immediate challenges of the present. We reflect on the significance of strategic foresight, the ability to anticipate and prepare for future uncertainties, and the importance of adapting our strategies in rapidly evolving environments.

To truly grasp Churchill's strategic leadership, we must delve into his actions during World War II, a time of unprecedented crisis. We analyze his capacity to make tough decisions that would shape the course of history. "I have nothing to offer but blood, toil, tears, and sweat," he famously declared, exemplifying his willingness to confront harsh realities head-on and his commitment to leading by example. Through meticulous examination, we extract valuable lessons from his decisive actions, learning how to cultivate the courage necessary to make difficult choices in our own leadership roles.

At the core of Churchill's strategic leadership was his ability to rally and inspire people even in the darkest of times. His iconic speeches, infused with unwavering resolve, became beacons of hope for a nation amidst the perils of war. We immerse ourselves in the power of his rhetoric, dissecting his communication strategies, and uncovering the secrets behind his ability to uplift and unite the spirits of those he led. His words, such as "We shall never surrender," reverberate through history as reminders of the transformative impact of strong and inspirational leadership.

Strategic leadership in the modern era encompasses a dynamic and rapidly changing landscape. We explore the complexities of decision-making in an interconnected world, where the consequences of choices ripple far beyond individual organizations or nations. Drawing from Churchill's wisdom, we learn how to balance short-term imperatives with long-term vision, ensuring that our decisions align with our strategic goals and values. Moreover, we delve into the importance of ethical leadership, exploring how to make principled choices that uphold integrity and foster trust.

In a world driven by data and technological advancements, we uncover the role of evidence-based decision-making in strategic leadership. Churchill's reliance on intelligence and sound analysis to inform his strategies and shape his policies becomes a guiding principle for us. We examine the importance of data-driven insights, embracing innovation, and adapting to the digital age while preserving the core principles of ethical leadership. By leveraging technology, gathering accurate information, and making informed decisions, we can navigate the complexities of our modern landscape.

Churchill's legacy reminds us that strategic leaders must also cultivate resilience and adaptability. "Success is not final, failure is not fatal: It is the courage to continue that counts," he famously stated. These words resonate deeply as we explore strategies for embracing change, learning from setbacks, and maintaining a steadfast focus on our goals despite obstacles. We delve into the power of resilience, the art of managing uncertainties, and the mindset needed to lead through turbulent times.

As we conclude this extensive and insightful chapter, we are reminded of the enduring impact of Churchill's strategic leadership. His visionary thinking, resolute decision-making, and unwavering determination provide invaluable lessons for navigating the complex challenges of our modern world. By harnessing the power of strategic thinking, adapting to change, and inspiring those around us, we can lead with conviction and guide our organizations and communities towards a brighter future.

To further enrich our understanding of strategic leadership, we draw upon actual quotes from Winston Churchill, allowing his words to illuminate our exploration. One of his notable quotes states, "Difficulties mastered are opportunities won." This profound insight underscores the importance of embracing challenges as opportunities for growth and innovation. We delve into the mindset required to transform obstacles into stepping stones and explore strategies for reframing difficulties as catalysts for positive change.

Churchill's strategic leadership was rooted in a comprehensive understanding of the geopolitical landscape. He recognized the interconnectedness of nations and the need for collaborative approaches. "The price of greatness is responsibility," he famously remarked, highlighting the importance of shouldering responsibility as a strategic leader. We examine the significance of global leadership in the modern era, navigating geopolitical complexities, and forging alliances that promote peace, stability, and prosperity.

In an era defined by rapid technological advancements, strategic leaders must navigate the intricacies of the digital realm. Churchill's insightful quote, "We are all worms, but I do believe I am a glowworm," inspires us to embrace innovation and harness the power of technology. We explore how strategic leaders can leverage digital tools, harness data analytics, and adapt to the evolving technological landscape to gain a competitive edge and drive organizational success.

Strategic leadership demands a forward-thinking approach that anticipates and prepares for future challenges. Churchill's words, "The future is unknowable, but the past should give us hope," encourage us to learn from history while remaining adaptable to change. We delve into the art of scenario planning, strategic foresight, and risk management, equipping leaders with the tools to navigate uncertainties, identify emerging trends, and position their organizations for long-term success.

Furthermore, effective strategic leadership requires the ability to inspire and mobilize teams toward a shared vision. "Success is not final, failure is not fatal: It is the courage to continue that counts," Churchill once said. We explore the art of visionary leadership, cultivating a compelling vision, and empowering individuals to contribute their best. Through fostering a culture of trust, collaboration, and shared purpose, strategic leaders can create environments that foster creativity, innovation, and high-performance.

As we conclude this chapter on strategic leadership, we are left with a deep sense of admiration for Winston Churchill's legacy. His strategic acumen, unwavering resolve, and inspirational leadership continue to resonate in the modern world. By embracing the lessons he imparted, we can navigate the complexities of our times, overcome challenges, and forge a path toward a brighter future.

CHAPTER 6
Leading with Integrity: Ethics and Values in the Spotlight

In this pivotal chapter, we delve deep into the essence of Winston Churchill's leadership by exploring his unwavering commitment to integrity and ethical conduct. Churchill's remarkable legacy serves as a timeless reminder of the importance of leading with a strong moral compass. As we examine his leadership journey, we uncover profound insights into the significance of ethical decision-making and the enduring impact of accountability in the modern world. Churchill's resolute dedication to upholding moral principles resonates powerfully with leaders of today. He believed that "the price of greatness is responsibility," emphasizing the inherent connection between leadership and ethical stewardship. We reflect upon the timeless wisdom contained within this statement, contemplating the profound responsibility that leaders bear in influencing the lives of individuals and the trajectory of organizations.

Throughout his career, Churchill demonstrated unwavering integrity in the face of challenging circumstances. His words, "Never give in, never give in, never, never, never, never—in nothing, great or small, large or petty—never give in except to convictions of honor and good sense," exemplify his steadfast adherence to his core values. We delve into the significance of staying true to one's principles and the importance of aligning actions with ethical beliefs in leadership roles.

In the modern world, ethical decision-making is paramount for leaders to earn trust, inspire loyalty, and foster a positive organizational culture. We examine the complex ethical dilemmas that leaders often face, navigating the intricacies of competing interests and conflicting values. Drawing inspiration from Churchill's resolute character, we explore strategies for ethical decision-making, emphasizing the need for empathy, fairness, and a commitment to the greater good.

Accountability is a cornerstone of ethical leadership, ensuring that leaders take responsibility for their actions and decisions. Churchill understood the weight of accountability when he said, "The price of greatness is responsibility." We explore the significance of holding oneself accountable, promoting transparency, and cultivating a culture of accountability within organizations. By leading by example and embracing accountability, leaders inspire trust, foster a sense of ownership, and promote a culture of integrity.

In an era where ethical lapses can have far-reaching consequences, it is essential for leaders to demonstrate unwavering ethical conduct. We examine the importance of ethical leadership in building sustainable organizations, fostering employee engagement, and maintaining stakeholder trust. By prioritizing ethics and values, leaders can navigate complex challenges, build resilient organizations, and create a positive impact on society. Moreover, ethical leadership extends beyond organizational boundaries. Leaders have a responsibility to address societal challenges and contribute to the greater good. We explore how Churchill's commitment to public service and his unwavering moral compass guided his actions during critical moments in history. By drawing inspiration from his legacy, we discover avenues for leaders to drive positive change, advocate for justice, and promote ethical leadership on a broader scale.

As we conclude this chapter, we are reminded of the profound influence of ethical leadership in the modern world. By embracing integrity, making ethical decisions, and fostering a culture of accountability, leaders can leave a lasting impact on individuals, organizations, and society as a whole. Join us in the next chapter as we continue to uncover the wisdom of Winston Churchill and his blueprint for leading in the modern world.

CHAPTER 7
Embracing Change: Adapting and Innovating in a Rapidly Evolving World

In this transformative chapter, we embark on a profound exploration of Winston Churchill's remarkable ability to embrace change and foster innovation in the face of a rapidly evolving world. Churchill's adaptability and forward-thinking mindset serve as a beacon of inspiration for leaders navigating the complexities of the modern era. As we delve deeper into his legacy, we uncover invaluable strategies for embracing change, driving innovation, and positioning ourselves for success in an ever-changing landscape.

Churchill's words resonate powerfully as we contemplate the importance of embracing change. He famously said, "To improve is to change; to be perfect is to change often." This insightful quote underscores his understanding that adaptability is not merely a desirable trait but an essential aspect of effective leadership. We reflect on the significance of a growth mindset, the willingness to challenge the status quo, and the courage to embark on new paths of innovation.

Throughout his life, Churchill demonstrated a remarkable ability to pivot and adapt to shifting circumstances. His leadership during World War II, where he guided Britain through one of its most challenging periods, stands as a testament to his ability to lead in times of uncertainty. By studying his strategic decisions and visionary thinking, we glean valuable insights into embracing change and driving transformative outcomes.

In the modern era, change is constant, and leaders must navigate through an ever-evolving landscape. We delve into strategies for embracing change, understanding its implications, and capitalizing on the opportunities it presents. By fostering a culture that encourages agility, continuous learning, and a willingness to adapt, leaders can position their organizations at the forefront of innovation and secure long-term success.

Innovation is the lifeblood of progress, and Churchill's visionary leadership exemplifies the transformative power of groundbreaking ideas. His quote, "We shape our buildings, and afterwards, our buildings shape us," emphasizes the importance of creating an environment that fosters innovation. Drawing from his legacy, we uncover strategies for driving innovation in the modern era, such as fostering a culture of experimentation, promoting interdisciplinary collaboration, and embracing emerging technologies.

Furthermore, we examine the role of leadership in creating an ecosystem that fosters innovation. Churchill's words inspire us to adopt an optimistic mindset and view challenges as opportunities for growth and innovation. We explore techniques for fostering a culture of innovation, such as empowering employees, promoting diversity of thought, and creating spaces for exploration and ideation.

Effective leadership in times of change requires a delicate balance between stability and transformation. We delve into strategies for managing change, ensuring organizational stability during transitions, and effectively communicating change initiatives to inspire and engage stakeholders. By honing our change leadership skills, we can guide our teams through periods of uncertainty, instill confidence, and foster a sense of purpose and direction.

As we continue to uncover Churchill's insights on embracing change and driving innovation, we are reminded of the profound relevance of his teachings in the modern world. By embracing change, nurturing a culture of innovation, and positioning ourselves as catalysts for transformation, we can navigate the complexities of the modern era and drive positive change in our organizations and communities.

CHAPTER 8
Resilient Leadership: Nurturing Mental Well-being in High-Stress Environments

In this pivotal chapter, we embark on a profound exploration of Winston Churchill's extraordinary resilience in the face of immense pressure and the paramount importance of nurturing mental well-being in high-stress leadership roles. Churchill's unwavering determination and fortitude serve as a guiding light for modern leaders, reminding us of the significance of prioritizing our mental health amidst demanding environments. As we delve deeper into this critical topic, we uncover invaluable techniques and insights for maintaining mental well-being and effectively managing stress, drawing inspiration from Churchill's own experiences and wisdom.

Churchill's iconic speech, where he spoke about fighting on the beaches, stands as a testament to his indomitable spirit in times of adversity. The weight of the world rested on his shoulders, and yet, he exhibited unwavering resolve and rallied his nation with his words. Examining this speech and the context surrounding it, we gain profound insights into Churchill's mental resilience and his ability to inspire and lead during the darkest of times. We reflect on the power of his words and the impact they had on the collective psyche, instilling a sense of resilience and fortitude in the face of daunting challenges.

Leadership roles often come with intense pressure and constant demands. In this chapter, we delve into the strategies employed by Churchill to maintain his mental well-being amidst the tremendous stress he faced. We explore his approach to self-care, recognizing that in order to lead effectively, one must prioritize their own well-being. Churchill found solace in activities such as painting, writing, and indulging in hobbies that provided an outlet for creativity and personal expression. He sought respite in nature, finding solace in the serenity of landscapes and the rejuvenating effects of being outdoors. Furthermore, he cherished quality time with loved ones, recognizing the importance of nurturing relationships as a source of support and emotional well-being. These examples highlight the multifaceted nature of self-care and the importance of finding balance in our lives as leaders.

Managing stress effectively is paramount for resilient leadership. In this chapter, we explore techniques for managing stress and building resilience in high-stress environments. Churchill's ability to maintain composure in the face of adversity provides valuable lessons in stress management. We delve into practices such as mindfulness and meditation, which can help leaders cultivate mental well-being and enhance their ability to handle challenging situations with clarity and grace. Regular exercise, with its numerous physical and mental health benefits, is also a vital component of stress management. Additionally, we discuss the importance of setting boundaries, managing workload, and embracing strategies for time management, all of which contribute to reducing stress and fostering a healthier work-life balance.

Furthermore, we examine the significance of fostering a supportive and positive work culture that prioritizes the well-being of team members. Churchill recognized the importance of a united and resilient team, and we draw inspiration from his leadership style. We explore strategies for creating a supportive environment, including promoting open communication, providing resources for mental health support, and fostering a culture of empathy and understanding. By nurturing an environment where individuals feel supported and valued, leaders can create a foundation for mental well-being and resilience.

Leadership is a marathon, not a sprint, and prioritizing mental well-being is crucial for sustained success. As we expand our understanding of Churchill's indomitable spirit and his unwavering commitment to his own well-being amidst the tumultuous times he faced, we are compelled to reflect on our own practices. By drawing from his example and embracing techniques for maintaining mental well-being, we can build resilience, enhance our decision-making capabilities, and lead with clarity, compassion, and strength.

Join us in the final chapter as we bring together the invaluable lessons from Winston Churchill's life and distill them into a powerful conclusion that will inspire and empower leaders in the modern world.

In the face of ever-increasing demands and rapidly evolving challenges, the importance of nurturing mental well-being cannot be overstated. Churchill's unwavering resilience and commitment to his own mental health provide timeless lessons for leaders today. By prioritizing mental well-being, leaders can not only enhance their own effectiveness but also create a culture of well-being and resilience within their organizations. As we navigate the complexities of the modern world, the ability to adapt and thrive in high-stress environments is crucial. Churchill's example reminds us of the power of resilience, as he faced seemingly insurmountable odds and emerged victorious. Leaders must embrace change and cultivate a forward-thinking mindset, seeking innovative solutions and remaining agile in the face of uncertainty.

Moreover, ethical leadership and integrity remain pillars of effective leadership. Churchill's unwavering commitment to his values and the greater good serves as a shining example for leaders today. By upholding ethical standards and making principled decisions, leaders can inspire trust, foster collaboration, and create a positive impact on society.

The journey of leadership is not without its challenges, and the mental well-being of leaders is often tested. By embracing self-care practices and prioritizing mental health, leaders can sustain their resilience and navigate the inevitable highs and lows with grace. Churchill's dedication to activities outside of his leadership role reminds us that true leadership encompasses more than just work—it embraces personal growth, creative expression, and nurturing relationships.

In conclusion, the lessons from Winston Churchill's remarkable life provide a blueprint for leadership in the modern world. From perseverance and courageous decision-making to effective communication and building cohesive teams, Churchill's legacy offers invaluable guidance for leaders and entrepreneurs. By drawing upon his experiences, incorporating his strategies, and adapting them to the demands of the modern era, leaders can forge a path of success and make a positive impact in their organizations and beyond.

Now, as we approach the final chapter, we stand on the precipice of a transformative conclusion. Join us as we distill the essence of Churchill's wisdom and inspire leaders to embark on their own journeys of growth, resilience, and impactful leadership.

CHAPTER 9
Legacy and Impact: Leaving a Lasting Mark on the Future

As we approach the culmination of our profound exploration into the life lessons of Winston Churchill, we immerse ourselves in the profound concept of legacy and the enduring impact that awaits us in the modern world. Churchill's extraordinary legacy transcends time, continuing to inspire generations, and stands as a testament to the power of purpose-driven leadership and the lasting imprint that one individual can leave on the world. In this final chapter, we embark on a deeper reflection of Churchill's legacy and embark on a journey to uncover ways in which we can create our own meaningful and enduring mark on the future.

Churchill's impact on history is indubitable. His indomitable spirit and unwavering resolve guided his nation through the darkest of times, leaving an indelible mark on the pages of history. From his eloquent speeches that ignited hope and determination in the hearts of the British people to his strategic leadership during World War II, Churchill's legacy reverberates through the annals of time, reminding us of the immense influence that one individual can have on the course of events. In this chapter, we delve even deeper into the multifaceted elements that contributed to Churchill's lasting impact, including his visionary foresight, unwavering determination, and the remarkable ability to inspire and unite people in pursuit of a greater cause.

However, what does legacy truly mean for leaders in the modern world? How can we leave an indelible mark on the future that echoes through the generations? As we navigate the intricacies of the 21st century, we are compelled to redefine the concept of legacy, embracing a broader understanding of our impact. It is no longer solely measured by grand achievements or historical significance; instead, it is about the positive influence we have on the lives of others, the meaningful contributions we make to society, and the legacy of positive change we leave behind.

Creating a profound and enduring legacy commences with a profound sense of purpose. In this chapter, we delve into the paramount importance of aligning our actions with our deepest values and vision, ensuring that every decision and endeavor is driven by a higher purpose. Churchill's unwavering commitment to his principles serves as an illuminating beacon, showcasing how leadership guided by a resolute moral compass can shape the future for the betterment of all.

Furthermore, we delve into the instrumental role of mentorship and the art of inspiring others in the intricate process of building a legacy. Churchill's indomitable spirit and unwavering resolve ignited the spark of inspiration in countless individuals, propelling them to rise to their full potential and become catalysts for positive change. We explore invaluable strategies for nurturing talent, empowering others, and fostering a culture of growth and development within organizations. By investing in the success of others, leaders can amplify their impact and leave behind a legacy that extends far beyond their own individual achievements.

Moreover, we embark on an exploration of the transformative power of innovation and the vital importance of embracing change as an avenue to create a lasting legacy. Churchill himself was unafraid to challenge the status quo, constantly embracing new ideas and steering his nation through times of profound transformation. We discuss the significance of cultivating a culture of innovation and adaptation, encouraging curiosity, and embracing calculated risks. By embracing change and pushing the boundaries of what is possible, leaders can foster a legacy of progress and inspire others to follow suit.

Finally, we turn our gaze towards the vital significance of collaboration and collective impact in constructing a lasting legacy. Churchill, with his unparalleled understanding of the strength of unity and the power of bringing diverse voices together, showcased the extraordinary outcomes that can arise from collaboration. We explore the inherent value of collaboration in the modern world, highlighting the potential for collective efforts to drive profound change and create a legacy that transcends the limitations of individual achievements. We delve deeper into the importance of fostering a culture of collaboration, cultivating trust, and leveraging the diverse perspectives and talents of teams. By embracing collaboration as a strategic tool, leaders can harness the collective power of their organization or community to tackle complex challenges and leave a lasting legacy of transformative change.

As we draw closer to the conclusion of our exploration of Churchill's life lessons and the path to leaving a lasting mark on the future, we are reminded that legacy is not confined to the confines of history books or the remembrance of great deeds. It is an ongoing journey, shaped by our actions, values, and the impact we have on others. It is a testament to the transformative power of our choices, the resilience we display in the face of adversity, and the unwavering commitment to making a positive difference.

Now, as we approach the final pages of this remarkable journey, I invite you to take a moment to reflect on the lessons learned, the inspiration gained, and the profound possibilities that lie ahead. How will you embrace your unique abilities and leadership potential to create a legacy that resonates with the needs of our time? How will you lead with integrity, inspire others, and cultivate collaboration to leave an indelible mark on the future? The path to a lasting legacy awaits, and it is within your reach to shape a future that echoes with the values and principles you hold dear.

As we bid farewell to the captivating tale of Winston Churchill, let us carry his legacy within us, as a reminder of the power we possess to shape the world around us. The time has come for you to embark on your own journey of leadership and impact, armed with the timeless wisdom of Churchill and the determination to leave a lasting mark on the future. The world awaits the imprint of your legacy, and I have no doubt that you will rise to the occasion with unwavering courage, resilience, and the unwavering commitment to making a difference.

In the final turn of this chapter, we leave you with a cliffhanger, eagerly anticipating the grand unveiling of the legacy you will create. The next chapter in your life's story beckons, and as you turn the page, remember the words of Winston Churchill: "We shape our buildings, and afterward, our buildings shape us." How will you shape the world, and how will the world, in turn, shape you? The answers lie within, waiting to be discovered as you forge ahead on your remarkable journey of leadership, impact, and legacy.

The end of this book marks the beginning of your own extraordinary story. Embrace it. Embody it. And let your legacy be written in the hearts and minds of those who come after you. The time is now.